THE SUN

BY HOLLY DUHIG

©2018
Book Life
King's Lynn
Norfolk PE30 4LS

ISBN: 978-1-78637-219-2

Written by:
Holly Duhig
Edited by:
Kirsty Holmes
Designed by:
Danielle Rippengill

A catalogue record for this book
is available from the British Library

PHOTO CREDITS

Abbreviations: l-left, r-right, b-bottom, t-top, c-centre, m-middle.

CONTENTS

Words that look like *this* are explained in the glossary on page 31.

WHAT IS THE SUN?

We see the Sun rise and set every day. It keeps us warm in summer and lights up the Earth during the daytime. But what exactly is the Sun?

The Sun is a star and, like all stars, it is an incredibly hot ball of burning gases in space. The temperature on the surface of the Sun is 5,000°C but its core can reach temperatures of 13,600000°C! The Sun is the centre of our Solar System. The Solar System is the name for the Sun and all the moons and planets, including Earth, that orbit it.

It takes Earth 365 days to orbit the Sun. We call this a year.

The Sun

The Sun looks much bigger than the other stars we can see in the night sky but this is only because it is much closer to us than they are. We can't see the other stars in the daytime because our Sun lights up the sky making it too bright to see anything else.

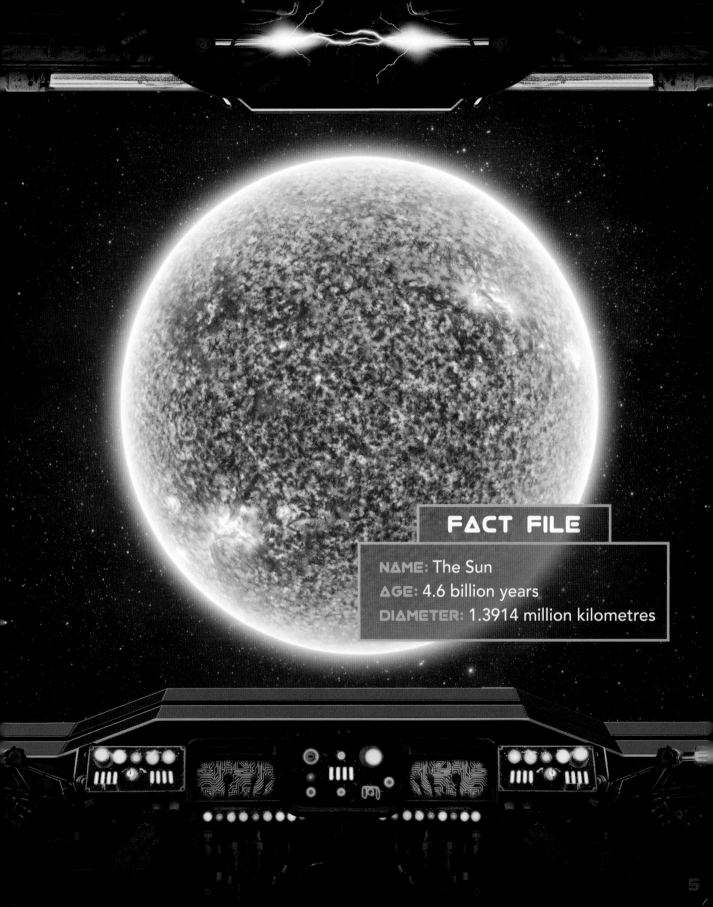

FACT FILE

NAME: The Sun
AGE: 4.6 billion years
DIAMETER: 1.3914 million kilometres

WHERE IS THE SUN?

The planets in our Solar System orbit the Sun because its gravity is very strong and pulls the planets towards it. The closest planet to the Sun is Mercury and the farthest away is Neptune.

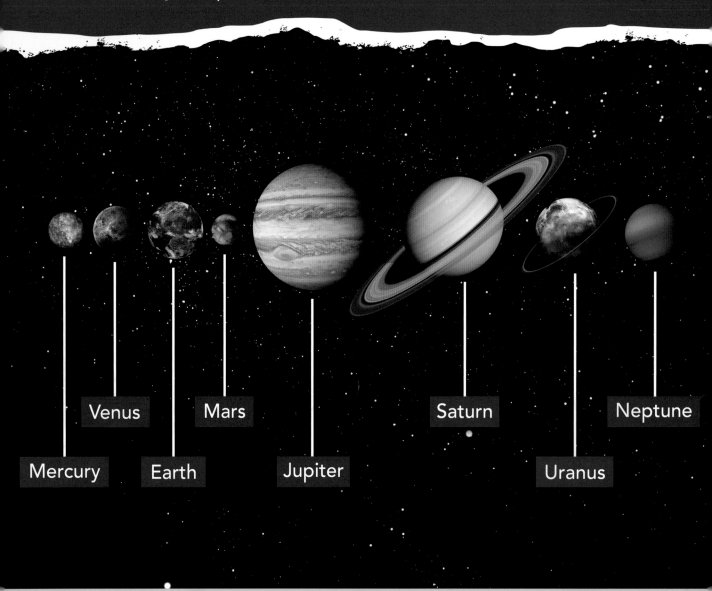

Venus

Mars

Saturn

Neptune

Mercury

Earth

Jupiter

Uranus

Our Solar System is part of a galaxy called the Milky Way. A galaxy is a group of stars and planets that are held in place by gravity and orbit a black hole. The Milky Way contains billions of stars and solar systems besides our own.

The Milky Way is about 100,000 lightyears wide and is shaped like a big spiral. Our own Sun can be found on one of the outer arms of this spiral. Our galaxy spins at speeds of over 800,000 kilometres per hour which means that, even though the Sun stays in the same position within our Solar System, it is flying through space at tremendous speeds.

There are billions of galaxies in the universe. Each one contains billions of stars.

Our Sun is on the outer edge of the Milky Way.

HOW DID THE SUN GET THERE?

1. Our Sun began its life as a cloud of gases and dust in space called a nebula. This cloud was mostly made of the gases hydrogen and helium, which might have been left over from the death of another star.

2. Gravity caused this cloud to collapse in on itself and form a flat disk, like a pancake.

1.

2.

4.

3.

This whole process would have taken millions of years.

3. Over time, the temperature and *pressure* of the gases at the centre of the disk increased and formed a ball shape. This ball eventually became the Sun.

4. Inside the ball, hydrogen *atoms* joined together in a process called nuclear fusion. This process releases huge amounts of energy and is what keeps the Sun burning.

THE PLANETS

As well as the Sun, this process formed all the planets in our Solar System, including planet Earth. Dust and rock in the outer edges of the disk would have kept colliding until they had formed planet-sized objects.

Small, dim stars are called red dwarfs. They can keep burning for trillions of years!

BIG STARS AND SMALL STARS

All stars are formed in this way. However, the process is slightly different each time. Big stars are formed quickly out of lots of gas whereas small stars, like our Sun, are made slowly out of much less gas. The formation of a star affects its lifespan. Big stars will have a shorter life than small stars because they have more fuel which causes the star to burn itself out more quickly.

WHAT IS OUR SUN MADE OF?

Our Sun may look like one giant ball of fire but it actually has many different layers.

The Sun's corona is its outermost layer. It is a layer of *plasma* that is millions of kilometres deep. The corona can only be seen from Earth during a solar eclipse because, usually, the rest of the Sun is so bright that we cannot see it. You can learn more about eclipses on page 16.

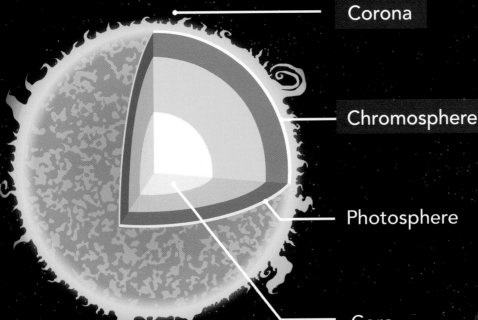

Corona

Chromosphere

Photosphere

Core

Corona

Solar Flare

Beyond the corona is the chromosphere. This is where explosions, called solar flares, take place. Solar flares can be ten times the size of Earth.

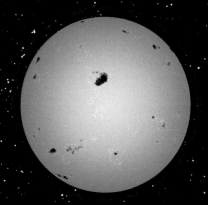

PHOTOSPHERE

This is the very thin, but very bright, part of the Sun that we can see from Earth. The whole Sun is 700,000 kilometres deep which makes the 100-kilometre-deep photosphere very thin indeed.

CORE

The innermost part of the Sun is its core. This is where most of the Sun's activity happens. The core is where the violent process of nuclear fusion takes place which produces all of the Sun's energy and keeps it burning bright.

It takes light from the Sun eight minutes and twenty seconds to reach Earth.

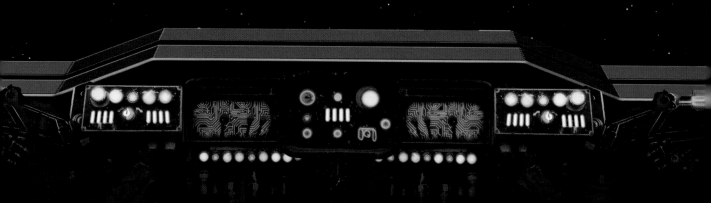

HOW DOES THE SUN AFFECT US?

Living things on Earth need the Sun in order to survive. The leaves of a plant use energy from the Sun to make food for the rest of the plant in a process called photosynthesis. Plants provide energy for animals and humans when eaten. Without this energy, living things – including humans – could not survive.

Wearing sun cream can stop you from getting sunburnt.

Sunlight also helps our skin to make vitamin D, which helps to keep our muscles and bones strong and healthy. However, too much sunlight on our skin can be a bad thing. The Sun's rays can give us sunburn and can even permanently damage our skin.

DAY AND NIGHT

On Earth, it looks like the Sun moves across the sky, but it is actually Earth that is moving. The Earth does one full rotation every 24 hours. We call this a day.

When the side of the Earth we live on is facing the Sun it will be daytime and when it faces away from the Sun it will be night-time. If the Earth didn't rotate, the one side of the planet that faced away from the Sun would always be cold and dark, and no plants would be able to grow there.

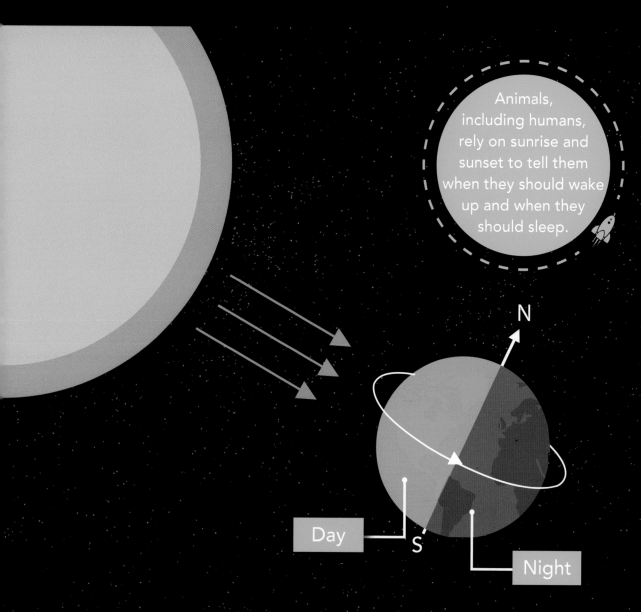

Animals, including humans, rely on sunrise and sunset to tell them when they should wake up and when they should sleep.

N

Day

S

Night

GLOBAL WARMING

When heat from the Sun hits the Earth, some of it gets trapped in the gases that make up the Earth's *atmosphere* and the rest is released back into space. This keeps our planet at the perfect temperature. However, in recent years, our planet has been getting hotter because of a harmful process called global warming.

Global warming happens when we burn *fossil fuels*. Burning fossil fuels creates energy that we use to fuel cars, power factories and heat our homes among many other things. However, burning fossil fuels releases other harmful gases, such as carbon dioxide, into the atmosphere. These gases are called greenhouse gases because – just like a greenhouse – they trap the Sun's heat. When this heat is trapped in the Earth's atmosphere it causes the temperature of Earth to increase.

SOLAR ENERGY

This change in temperature can cause lots of problems, such as habitat destruction, rising sea levels and flooding. If temperatures keep getting higher, life might not be able to survive on Earth. However, there are ways of making electricity that don't produce greenhouse gases. For example, solar panels use light from the Sun to make electricity.

Solar Panels

Solar panels make use of materials that, when exposed to sunlight, produce an electric current. These materials are connected to metal *conductors* that carry the spark of electricity to where it is needed. This method of producing electricity does not harm the planet.

ECLIPSES

Just like the Earth orbits the Sun, the Moon orbits the Earth. From time to time the Moon will move between the Sun and the Earth. This stops the Sun's light from reaching our planet. We call this a solar eclipse.

Never look directly at a solar eclipse. It might look dark, but the Sun's rays can still damage your eyes.

Solar eclipses happen very rarely. Only a few people will be lucky enough to see a total solar eclipse during their lifetime. Only the small part of the Earth that is completely in the Moon's shadow will experience a total solar eclipse. The rest of the world will either see a partial eclipse, where the sky goes a bit darker, or nothing at all.

VIEWING A SOLAR ECLIPSE

Even though you should not look directly at a solar eclipse, there are still safe ways of viewing them. One way to view an eclipse is through a pinhole projector.

TO MAKE ONE OF THESE YOU WILL NEED:

Two Paper Plates
One Pin

1. Make a hole in one of the paper plates with a pin. Make sure the hole is smooth and round.

2. During an eclipse, stand with your back towards the Sun and hold the paper plate with the pinhole up to the Sun.

3. Hold the second paper plate in front of the other so that the sunlight that shines through the pinhole is *projected* onto it.

Sun

Moon

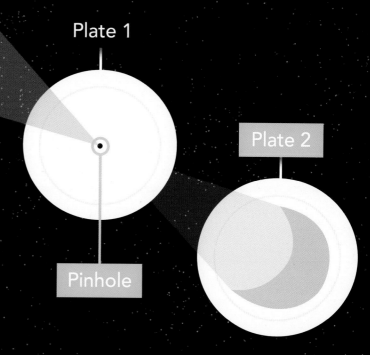

Plate 1

Plate 2

Pinhole

Top Tip!
Ask an adult or teacher to help you make your pinhole projector.

An image of the Sun will be projected onto the second plate and you will be able to see the Moon's shadow as it passes across the Sun.

BEAUTIFUL SUN

The Sun can cause many amazing natural phenomena on Earth, for example, rainbows. We can often see rainbows in the sky when the Sun comes out while it is still raining. This is because rainbows are caused by sunlight shining through raindrops in the air.

White light, like the light we get from the Sun or a lightbulb, is actually made up of all the different colours of the rainbow; red, orange, yellow, green, blue, indigo and violet. Raindrops split the Sun's light into all these different colours, so we can see them.

AURORAS

Auroras – often nicknamed the northern or southern lights – are colourful lights that can be seen lighting up the sky in both of the **polar regions**. These lights might look magical and mysterious but they are actually caused by solar winds.

In Norse *mythology*, the northern lights were believed to be a rainbow bridge connecting our world to the *afterlife*.

The Northern Lights

Solar winds are streams of plasma and particles from the Sun which are projected into outer space. When the particles in solar winds interact with the Earth's *magnetic field* and the gases in its atmosphere, colourful lights are produced.

STARS IN THE UNIVERSE

TYPES OF STAR

There are many different stars of all different sizes, colours and temperatures in the universe. Just like the hottest part of a flame glows blue, the hottest stars also tend to be blue in colour. Cooler stars tend to be yellow or red just like the cooler tip of a flame.

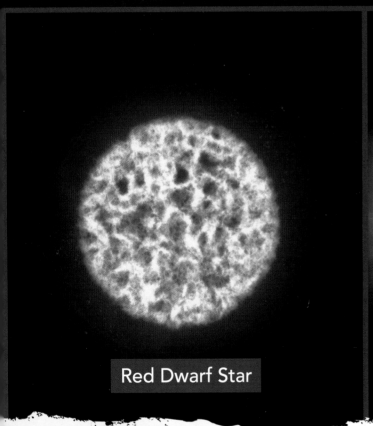

Red Dwarf Star

Blue Supergiant

A red dwarf star is a very small type of star. It glows red because it does not have enough fuel to keep it as hot. Blue supergiants are the biggest (as well as the hottest) type of star.

The size and colour of a star can tell us a lot about its lifespan. Blue stars have the shortest lifespans because they burn up their fuel much faster than other stars. Red dwarf stars have the longest lifespans and can keep burning for trillions of years.

Our own Sun – a yellow dwarf – has a lifespan of ten billion years but it is already middle-aged and only has about five billion years left.

DOUBLE TROUBLE!

Some stars orbit other stars. This creates what is called a binary star system. The two stars in a binary system are often formed out of the same nebula. However, sometimes a big star will pull a smaller star into its orbit.

LIFE CYCLE OF A STAR
SMALL STARS

1. A star is born when a cloud of gas and dust begins to collapse in on itself.
2. The star spends its life creating light and heat energy by fusing hydrogen atoms to make helium.
3. The star runs out of hydrogen and expands to form a red giant.
4. The red giant collapses and becomes a white dwarf.

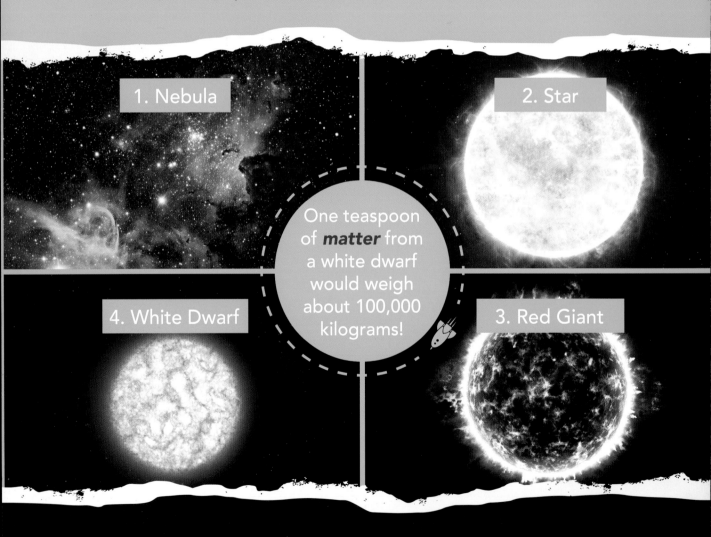

1. Nebula

2. Star

One teaspoon of **matter** from a white dwarf would weigh about 100,000 kilograms!

4. White Dwarf

3. Red Giant

A white dwarf is very small and very *dense*. When our Sun dies and becomes a white dwarf, it will be about the size of Earth but will weigh the same as it does now.

supergiants but their cores become so dense and heavy that they blow up in a giant explosion called a supernova. A supernova is so powerful that it can outshine an entire galaxy of stars.

After the explosion, what's left of the core shrinks to become a neutron star or a black hole. Neutron stars are very small, fast-spinning stars. Black holes are dark spheres which have such a strong gravity that they pull all nearby objects into them. Even light cannot escape!

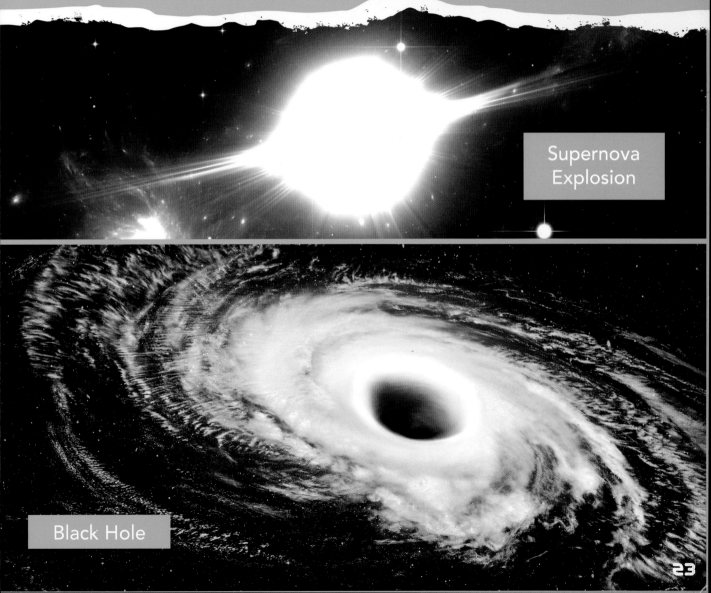

Supernova
Explosion

Black Hole

CONSTELLATIONS

Constellations are groups of stars that form patterns in the night sky. Most constellations were discovered and named many centuries ago.

ORION

This constellation was named after a skilled hunter in Greek mythology. You might have looked up at the night sky at some point and seen three bright stars in a row. These are said to be Orion's belt.

SCORPIO

Scorpio is supposed to represent the scorpion that was sent to kill Orion. Orion and Scorpio are never seen in the sky at the same time as each other. This is said to be because Orion is always running away from Scorpio.

Orion's Belt

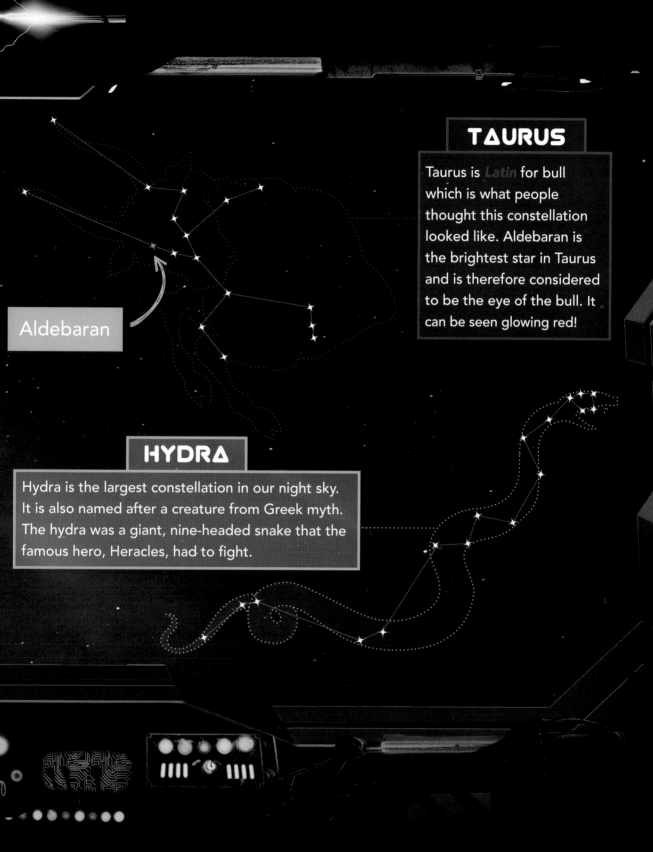

TAURUS

Taurus is *Latin* for bull which is what people thought this constellation looked like. Aldebaran is the brightest star in Taurus and is therefore considered to be the eye of the bull. It can be seen glowing red!

Aldebaran

HYDRA

Hydra is the largest constellation in our night sky. It is also named after a creature from Greek myth. The hydra was a giant, nine-headed snake that the famous hero, Heracles, had to fight.

SPECTACULAR STARS

UY SCUTI

UY Scuti is one of the biggest stars we know of. It is said to be five billion times bigger than our Sun. If this giant star was at the centre of our Solar System, it would reach all the way out to Jupiter.

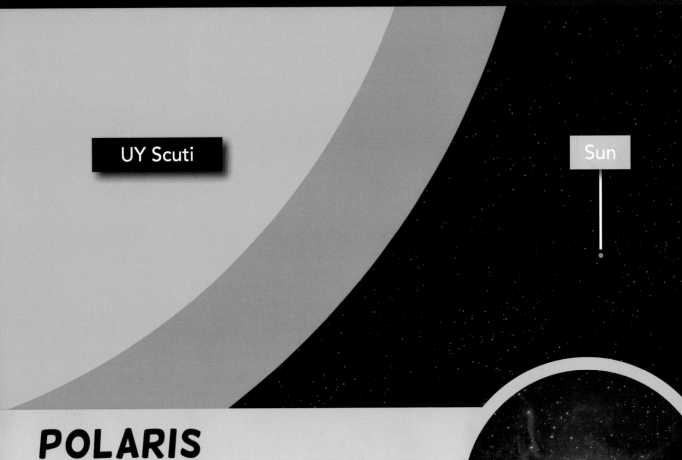

UY Scuti

Sun

POLARIS

Polaris is often known as the Northern Star because its position in the sky is above the North Pole. Because of this, it has been used for **navigation** for many centuries. It is found in the constellation Ursa Minor and is one of the brightest stars in the night sky if you live in the **Northern Hemisphere**.

SIRIUS

Sirius is the brightest star in our night sky. It is also the sixth closest star to our Sun and is travelling towards us at speeds of 7.6 kilometres per second! Don't worry though, our Sun is quite safe. Sirius is still about 8.6 lightyears away and one lightyear is equal to 9.5 trillion kilometres!

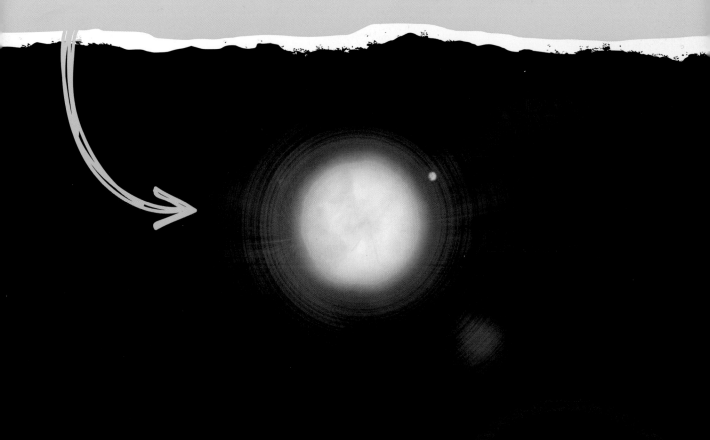

OGLE

OGLE, or OGLE-TR-122b to give it its full name, is the smallest star that scientists know of and is not much larger than Jupiter. Because it is so small and doesn't shine very brightly, it is called a brown dwarf.

ALIEN SUNS

Our Sun is the perfect temperature and distance away from Earth for life to flourish on our planet. However, there are billions more stars in just our galaxy alone – many with their own system of planets orbiting them. Could these solar systems be home to alien life?

TRAPPIST-1

The discovery of this star, and the planets that orbit it, has been very exciting for *astronomers*. TRAPPIST-1 is a red dwarf star. It does not give out much light or heat but the planets that orbit it are close enough to keep warm. If there is water and a thick atmosphere on any of these planets, they may well be the perfect home for alien life!

TABBY'S STAR

Tabby's Star is very far away. In fact, it is about 1,280 lightyears away from our Sun. However, this star got a whole lot more interesting when astronomers discovered that lots of small objects were orbiting it.

They had many ideas on what these objects could be. Some astronomers think the objects could be *debris* left over from a big event, such as the star swallowing a planet. However, one theory is that the objects are a structure built by an alien civilisation in order to collect energy from their star.

What do you think? Could alien life be out there orbiting alien suns?

QUICK QUIZ

How hot is the Sun's surface?

How long does it take light from the Sun to reach Earth?

What galaxy is our Solar System part of?

What is a solar flare?

What vitamin does sunlight help our bodies make?

What is global warming?

What is the real name for the northern and southern lights?

Which type of star has the shortest lifespan?

What happens to a big star when it dies?

Which constellation has three bright stars in a row?

Which constellation contains a star called Aldebaran?

Which star is the brightest star in our night sky?

GLOSSARY

°C	the symbol for degrees Celsius, the metric measurement of temperature
AFTERLIFE	a religious belief that there is life after death
ASTRONOMERS	people who study the universe and objects in space
ATMOSPHERE	the mixture of gases that make up the air and surround the Earth
ATOMS	the smallest particle of any substance that can possibly exist
CONDUCTORS	materials that let electricity flow through them
DEBRIS	the remains of something that has been broken
DENSE	tightly packed
FOSSIL FUELS	fuels, such as coal, oil and gas, that formed millions of years ago from the remains of animals and plants
GASES	air-like substances that expand freely to fill any space available
GRAVITY	the force that attracts physical bodies together and increases in strength as a body's mass increases
LATIN	the language of ancient Rome and its empire
LIFESPAN	how long something lives
MAGNETIC FIELD	a protective force around the world that is created by the liquid and solid cores of the Earth
MATTER	any material that has mass and takes up space
MYTHOLOGY	relating to, based on, or appearing in myths or mythology
NAVIGATION	finding your way around
NORTHERN HEMISPHERE	the half of the Earth that is north of the equator
ORBIT	the path that an object makes around a larger object in space
PHENOMENA	remarkable occurrences that are observed to exist or happen
PLASMA	a collection of charged particles that acts like a gas but can conduct electricity.
POLAR REGIONS	areas surrounding the north and south poles
PRESSURE	a continuous physical force exerted on an object, which is caused by something pressing against it
PROJECTED	pushed or thrown forward
ROTATION	turn around a central point or axis

INDEX